D1372435

CHILDREN IN
THE INDUSTRIAL
REVOLUTION

by Russell Roberts

FOCUS
READERS

www.focusreaders.com

Focus Readers is distributed by North Star Editions:
sales@northstareditions.com | 888-417-0195

Produced for Focus Readers by Red Line Editorial.

Content Consultant: John Fliter, Associate Professor of Political Science, Kansas State University

Photographs ©: Everett Historical/Shutterstock Images, cover, 1, 15; Joseph E.B. Elliot/Historic American Buildings Survey/Historic American Engineering Record/Historic American Landscapes Survey/Library of Congress, 4–5; Red Line Editorial, 6, 40; Lewis Wickes Hine/National Child Labor Committee Collection/Library of Congress, 8–9, 11, 13, 18, 20, 22–23, 25, 30–31, 33, 35; Detroit Publishing Company/Library of Congress, 16–17; National Photo Company Collection/Library of Congress, 27; Bain News Service/Bain Collection/Library of Congress, 29, 36–37, 42–43; Kansas State Historical Society, 39; Russell Lee/Farm Security Administration/Office of War Information/Library of Congress, 45

ISBN
978-1-63517-877-7 (hardcover)
978-1-63517-978-1 (paperback)
978-1-64185-181-7 (ebook pdf)
978-1-64185-080-3 (hosted ebook)

Library of Congress Control Number: 2018931673

Printed in the United States of America
Mankato, MN
May, 2018

ABOUT THE AUTHOR

Russell Roberts is an award-winning writer who has written and published more than 75 books for children and adults. Included among his books for adults are *Down the Jersey Shore* and *Rediscover the Hidden New Jersey*. Among his children's books are biographies, examinations of famous buildings, and stories about characters from Greek mythology.

TABLE OF CONTENTS

CHAPTER 1

A NATION TRANSFORMED

In the second half of the 1700s, the Industrial Revolution began in Great Britain. Before the revolution, most **manufacturing** happened in families' homes. But now, large machines in factories could produce goods faster and in greater amounts. This process was known as industrialization. Toward the end of the 1700s, the Industrial Revolution arrived in the United States.

The first successful US cotton factory was built in Pawtucket, Rhode Island, in 1793.

Before the revolution, most Americans' lives
revolved around farming. But now, millions of
workers moved to urban areas to work in factories.
Cities grew quickly. Increased immigration
to the United States also caused cities to

➤ IMMIGRANTS IN THE UNITED STATES

Top country of birth among US immigrants (1880)

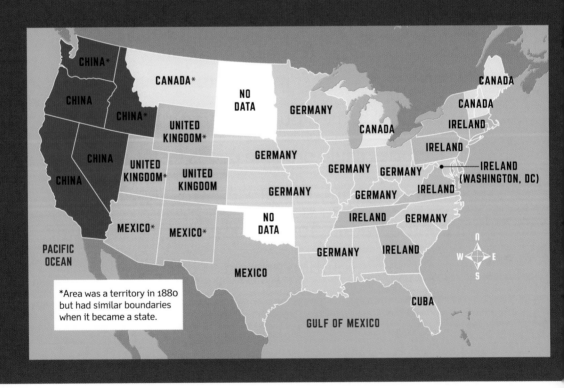

CHINA*
CANADA*
NO DATA
GERMANY
CANADA
CANADA
IRELAND
CHINA
CHINA*
UNITED KINGDOM*
CANADA
IRELAND
CHINA
UNITED KINGDOM*
UNITED KINGDOM
GERMANY
GERMANY
GERMANY
IRELAND
IRELAND (WASHINGTON, DC)
CHINA
GERMANY
GERMANY
IRELAND
MEXICO*
MEXICO*
NO DATA
IRELAND
GERMANY
PACIFIC OCEAN
MEXICO
GERMANY
IRELAND
W N E S
*Area was a territory in 1880 but had similar boundaries when it became a state.
MEXICO
CUBA
GULF OF MEXICO

grow. Between 1880 and 1920, the country's immigrant population rose from 7 million to nearly 14 million. Many immigrants found jobs in factories, including children.

As the Industrial Revolution grew, several states created child labor laws. These laws limited the hours that children could work. They also set a minimum working age for children. However, the laws were not strictly enforced. Some parents lied about their children's ages so they would be allowed to work.

By 1900, approximately 20 percent of US children had joined the workforce. Millions of children found jobs instead of going to school. They worked long hours in poor conditions to help support their families. Across the United States, in **mills**, mines, shipyards, and more, the children of the Industrial Revolution went to work.

CHAPTER 2

SPINNING COTTON

Child labor was not a new idea in the United States. In 1791, US Secretary of the Treasury Alexander Hamilton suggested that children could be a cheap source of labor for manufacturers. A national magazine called *Niles' Register* agreed, recommending that girls between the ages of 6 and 12 should perform factory work instead of adult men. In factories, young girls could fit in small spaces and between machines.

This young girl monitored two rows of cotton machinery at a mill in Newberry, South Carolina.

Textile mills were a common source of work for children, particularly in New England and the South. These mills produced large amounts of cotton textiles. Many textile mills hired children because they could pay them less than adults. Adults received six to seven dollars weekly, while children earned only two dollars per week.

Many children in mills worked as spinners and doffers. Children in these jobs watched the long rows of rapidly spinning spools. When thread broke, spinners had to quickly tie the two ends back together. When spools were full, doffers replaced them with empty ones.

> **THINK ABOUT IT**
>
> Why do you think children in the Industrial Revolution were paid less than adults?

▲ Doffers wheeled around carts of empty and full spools. The spools were also called bobbins.

Children typically worked 10 to 12 hours per day, often standing the entire time. If children fell asleep on the job, their supervisors would shout, shake, or even kick them awake. Some supervisors would throw cold water in their faces.

Children started work in the mills at a young age. For example, a six-year-old named Mattie worked in a narrow space next to a cotton spinner for 12 hours a day. As she worked, the constant roar of machinery filled her ears.

In a different mill, a five-year-old girl worked the entire day alongside her seven-year-old sister. Her hair was often covered with cotton thread. Another young mill worker, who weighed less than 50 pounds (23 kg), had to climb onto the machines to do her job. She worked all night, from 6:00 p.m. to 6:00 a.m.

Working conditions inside textile mills were horrible. Heat prevented cotton thread from breaking, so workers had to keep the windows closed. Meanwhile, lint from cotton filled the air and settled into children's lungs. This could cause serious illnesses such as tuberculosis and pneumonia. Mills also had poor lighting, dirty floors, and machinery that caused many injuries.

During the Industrial Revolution, children were twice as likely as adults to be hurt in an accident. In one mill, a 12-year-old doffer lost two fingers

△ Cotton covers a spinner's hair and clothes as she tends to her spools.

when he fell onto a set of gears. In Pennsylvania, boys younger than 10 reported losing parts of fingers and even entire hands in textile mills. The dangerous work even cost some workers their lives. Boys working in cotton mills were only half as likely to reach the age of 20, compared with boys who didn't work in mills. For girls, the odds were even worse.

CAMELLA TEOLI

Camella Teoli was 14 years old when she went on **strike** with nearly 30,000 mill workers in Lawrence, Massachusetts. Like other strikers, Camella wanted better working conditions and higher pay. She came from a poor family of Italian immigrants.

In March 1912, Camella spoke before the US Congress to bring more attention to the strike. "I used to go to school," Camella said, "and then a man came up to my house and asked my father why I didn't go to work, so my father says I don't know whether she is 13 or 14 years old. So, the man says you give me four dollars and I will make the papers come from the old country saying you are 14." One month later, Camella started work.

One day at the mill, Camella's hair got caught in a spinning machine. "The machine pulled the scalp off," she told the members of Congress.

▲ Many children participated in the Lawrence Textile Strike of 1912.

According to Camella, a friend found her scalp and wrapped it in newspaper. Camella spent seven months in the hospital before returning to work.

Camella's actions drew national attention. The workers won the strike and received a pay raise. A street in Lawrence, called Camella Teoli Way, now honors the young striker.

"Camella Teoli Testifies about the 1912 Lawrence Textile Strike." *History Matters*. American Social History Productions, Inc., n.d. Web. 8 Mar. 2018.

CHAPTER 3

BREAKER BOYS

As the Industrial Revolution wore on, photos slowly emerged of children's poor working conditions. One photographer, Lewis Hine, took thousands of photos of child laborers at work. Many of Hine's photos show boys with coal dust smeared on their faces. These children were called breaker boys, and they had one of the most dangerous jobs in the Industrial Revolution.

These breaker boys worked in the Woodward Coal Mines in Pennsylvania in approximately 1900.

▲ Thick coal dust made it difficult for breaker boys to do their jobs.

Breaker boys worked in breaker buildings. Here, heavy machinery broke big pieces of coal into smaller chunks. As chunks of coal whizzed by on conveyor belts, breaker boys searched for pieces that were not coal. If they spotted a piece of stone or slate, they had to reach in and pick it out.

The conveyer never stopped, so breaker boys had to move quickly. Supervisors struck boys with broom handles if they weren't watching closely enough. Boys who reached down too far could fall onto the coal and be seriously hurt or killed.

Breaker boys faced other dangers in the workplace as well. Many boys developed coughs from breathing in coal dust. Their backs ached from spending hours hunched over and staring down. And their fingers bled from handling sharp pieces of coal. New workers, whose fingers had not yet hardened, had bloodstained fingers. The breakers called the injured fingers *red tops*.

Another common job in the coal industry was the nipper. Nippers worked in mines, opening and closing doors to let cars full of coal pass through.

THINK ABOUT IT ◄

What do you think would be the worst part of working in a mine? Why?

 A nipper sits in a Pennsylvania mine, waiting on cars of coal.

For up to 10 hours per day, nippers sat in nearly total darkness, breathing in coal dust and oil fumes. They never moved except to open and close the door.

Children working in the coal industry faced disease, injury, and death. Still, miners' sons often couldn't wait to start working in mines. They thought working as nippers or breaker boys would begin their journey into adulthood. Many looked forward to becoming miners, just like their fathers.

Children who didn't work in factories or mines often found jobs in the food industry. Child labor laws did not apply to farmwork. So many children traveled from farm to farm with their families. They harvested cranberries, cotton, beets, and many other crops. Other children worked in canneries, where food was canned. In oyster canneries, children used sharp knives to pry open oyster shells. The shells caused the skin on their fingers to crack and bleed.

Many children working on farms or at canneries were recent immigrants to the United States. They rarely had the opportunity to attend school. Often, immigrant children had dreamed of living in the United States. Now, their dreams were replaced with long hours of hard work.

CHAPTER 4

WORKING FROM HOME

Not all child workers in the Industrial Revolution had jobs in factories or mines. Some children worked out of homes. However, in many cases, the working conditions in homes were just as bad as in factories.

Between 1800 and 1880, the population of New York City doubled every decade. Immigrants made up a large part of the population, but many of them had no place to live. The city was full.

Child workers take a break behind their home in New York City in the early 1900s.

Building owners divided single-family homes into living spaces for multiple families. These buildings were called tenements. By 1900, two-thirds of New York City's population was living in tenements. The buildings were cramped, dark, and poorly **ventilated**. As many as 12 people would sleep in the same small room.

Meanwhile, factories were springing up in the city. In one block, 77 factories employed a total of approximately 40,000 workers. Many tenements were located near the factories. This closeness made it easy for the factories to take some of their work to people who lived in tenements. The tenement workplaces that formed became known as the sweatshop industry.

Tenement owners, known as sweaters, used materials from factories to set up sweatshops in their buildings. Factories benefited from the

▲ This family sewed clothes in their cramped tenement, making one to two dollars per week.

arrangement. Sweatshop workers earned only one-third the pay of regular workers. A typical sweatshop was 10 by 40 feet (3 by 12 m) and contained 40 women, 10 men, and 12 children. In 1882, approximately 100,000 children in New York City worked in tenements. They worked 70 hours per week to earn only two dollars.

Children's tasks in sweatshops varied. Children sorted human hair for wigs, sewed doll clothes, and even helped roll tobacco into cigarettes.

Young girls helped their mothers sew buttons, collars, hems, linings, suits, coats, and more. Boys as young as 10 carried heavy bundles of fabric from factories to sweatshops.

Paper flowers were another common product made in sweatshops. A three-year-old girl named Angelica made 540 flowers daily to earn a total of five cents. Another girl didn't like being at home because it was filled with flowers. She preferred school, but she had little time for homework while making paper flowers.

The sweatshop industry changed on March 25, 1911. On that day, a fire erupted in the Triangle Shirtwaist Company in New York City. Of the 146 workers who died, 30 were under 18 years old. The state of New York passed 36 new laws because of the fire. One law barred children under the age of 14 from working in tenements. Another

A woman and children make paper flowers in a New York tenement.

law said children between the ages of 14 and 16 could work no more than 48 hours per week. They also couldn't work after 6:00 p.m., which meant no more overnight shifts.

Even though there were new restrictions, child labor in sweatshops continued. For tenement children of the Industrial Revolution, there was little difference between the factory and home. It was all work.

SADIE FROWNE

Before 1900, 10-year-old Sadie Frowne had lived in Poland with her family. But after her father died, Sadie and her mother moved to the United States. They wanted to start a new life. They traveled by boat as **steerage** passengers. Hundreds of other people were jammed in around them. Sadie said it was "a very dark place that smelt dreadfully."

Shortly after Sadie and her mother arrived in New York City, her mother died. To support herself, Sadie found a job at a sweatshop. She made shirts from 7:00 a.m. until 6:00 p.m. or later. One time, when she made a mistake, her supervisor called her "a stupid animal." Sadie had no choice but to continue working.

"The machines go like mad all day," Sadie said. "The faster you work, the more money you make." Sometimes, she worked so fast at her sewing machine that she put the needle right through

A group of immigrants arrives at the Ellis Island inspection station in New York.

her finger. "It goes so quick, though, that it does not hurt much," she said. "I bind the finger up with a piece of cotton and go on working." At the end of each day, all Sadie wanted to do was sleep. Instead, she forced herself to go dancing with friends. "You must . . . have some pleasure," she said.

Chaim M. Rosenberg. *Child Labor in America: A History.* Jefferson, NC: McFarland, 2013. Print. 81–82.

CHAPTER 5

ON THE STREET

Many child workers during the Industrial Revolution found jobs on the street. Several types of street jobs existed for these children, especially in large cities. Children shined shoes, delivered messages, ran errands, made deliveries, and sold goods such as candies and flowers.

In New York City, thousands of children, called newsies, sold newspapers on busy city streets.

A newsie in St. Louis, Missouri, tries to get the attention of customers.

The majority of these children were orphans living on the street or in crowded boarding houses. Newsies woke up in the middle of the night, when the newspapers were printed. They bought papers directly from the newspaper companies. Then they rushed to the streets, claimed a street corner, and began selling.

Newsies did not receive a weekly paycheck or wage. They made money only if they sold papers, and any papers they didn't sell cost them money. In the late 1800s, newsies would pay 65 cents for a stack of 100 newspapers. Then they sold the papers for one penny each. If they sold all their newspapers, they could make a total of 35 cents. However, selling this many newspapers could be difficult. Competition for the best street locations was fierce. Boys often fought one another to claim prime selling spots.

▲ Many young newsies did not know how to make change.

Newsies tried numerous tricks to make money. They would often shout false headlines to stir interest and attract potential customers. Many newsies would tell people that they were on their last paper and, if they sold it, they could go home. Once a person bought the paper and walked away, the newsie would pull out another paper and repeat the trick.

At the beginning of the 1900s, the average age of newsies was 12 years old. However, many were as young as five. Newsies worked in all types of weather. As a result, they often suffered from **respiratory** illnesses such as tuberculosis. Some newsies permanently damaged their legs and feet by standing on hard pavement for countless hours. Others would freeze to death while sleeping outside.

Street performing was another common job for children. Many child street performers were part of the **padrone** system. Padrones recruited children from Italy, promising them a bright future in the United States. However, when the children arrived, they were forced to work long hours performing on the street. After performing, they were forced to give all of their earnings to the padrone. If they refused, they would be beaten.

Many street workers, such as these three boys, could not read or write.

Adults often viewed newsies, street performers, and other child workers on the streets as young **merchants**. They thought the children would learn about business and go on to lead successful lives. However, in reality, the majority of these children would continue to live in poverty. Without an education or skills, they faced a bleak future.

CHAPTER 6

ORPHAN TRAINS

In the mid-1800s, between 10,000 and 30,000 homeless children lived on the streets of New York City. During the day, the children begged for food and money. At night, they took shelter under doorways. A minister named Charles Loring Brace was horrified by the children's living conditions. In an attempt to solve the problem, Brace founded the Children's Aid Society (CAS). CAS protested child labor and created schools for child workers.

Many charities tried to help orphans. Here, a group of orphans goes on an outing in New York.

In 1853, CAS announced that it would begin sending orphaned, abandoned, and neglected children in New York City to the Midwest on trains. Once there, the children would move in with farming families. Initially, this process was called "placing out." Today, it is known as the Orphan Train Movement.

CAS workers gathered children from boarding houses, orphanages, and street corners three times per month. If a child's parents were available, CAS received their legal permission to send the child away. Many parents hoped their children would find better lives in the Midwest.

The children selected for the orphan trains received new clothes and a Bible. CAS agents accompanied them on their trip. Most children enjoyed the excitement of the train ride, unaware of what was really happening. Others were

△ Children of all ages traveled across the United States on orphan trains.

anxious and worried about their future. Children who had left behind families didn't know if they would ever see their parents again.

The orphan trains were advertised in local Midwestern newspapers before arriving in towns. Once the children arrived, CAS agents would take them to a large public building. There, families could meet the children and bring them home.

Some families wanted a child to raise and take care of. Others wanted a worker who could do chores around the farm and house.

Children not selected by families returned to the train, to repeat the process in the next town.

A HOME ACROSS THE COUNTRY

Children placed by the Children's Aid Society (1854–1910)

NONE | 1–1,299 | 1,300–2,999 | 3,000–4,999 | 5,000–10,000 | MORE THAN 10,000

Those who were selected stayed with families on a trial basis. If children were unhappy at their new home, they could leave. Some children found good homes. For example, John Brady and Andrew Burke grew up to become state governors. Other children were not so lucky. Many children drifted from farm to farm, and some even made the trip back to New York City.

Approximately 3,000 children rode the orphan trains each year between 1855 and 1875. The majority of children selected for the program were born in the United States or had English, Irish, or German backgrounds. Between 1860 and 1890, less than 1 percent of CAS placements were Jewish or Italian children. Chinese, African American, Spanish, and Slavic children were also rarely placed. As a result, thousands of children continued to live on the streets.

CHAPTER 7

LET THEM PLAY AND LEARN

In 1904, activists formed the National Child Labor Committee (NCLC). The group hoped to end child labor. The NCLC enlisted the help of photographer Lewis Hine to help spread its message. Hine's photographs showed child workers who were exhausted and sick. After learning about the horrors of child labor, many parents and educators called for **reforms**.

Two girls protest child labor with signs that read, "Abolish child slavery!" in Yiddish and English.

By the early 1900s, most states had created stricter labor laws. These laws required children to attend the full school year until they were 17 years old. Between 1890 and 1900, high school enrollment increased by 150 percent. Education for younger children such as kindergartens also became more popular.

Many factory owners and workers fought against efforts to end child labor. In South Carolina, thousands of mill workers signed a **petition** against child labor reforms. The petition claimed that workers wanted to stay in their jobs. But dozens of the children in the petition did not

> THINK ABOUT IT

Why do you think some people were against ending child labor?

⚠ Child labor laws often did not apply to farming, so many children found work on farms in the 1900s.

know how to sign their names. They signed by writing an X instead.

By 1914, the Industrial Revolution had reached its peak. However, some forms of child labor continued. Even today, more than 153,600 American children work in violation of child labor laws each week. The Industrial Revolution may be over. But child labor practices, and the efforts to end them, are not.

CHILDREN IN THE INDUSTRIAL REVOLUTION

Write your answers on a separate piece of paper.

1. Write a sentence summarizing the main idea of Chapter 7.

2. Changing child labor laws in the United States took a long time. Why do you think this was the case?

3. Which type of worker spent time in mines?

    A. newsies
    B. padrones
    C. nippers

4. Why did some children on orphan trains return to New York City?

    A. They could not find good homes or families to stay with in the Midwest.
    B. Child labor reforms drew them back to their previous jobs.
    C. CAS agents forced them to return.

Answer key on page 48.

GLOSSARY

manufacturing
The making of goods by manual labor or machinery.

merchants
People who buy goods and sell them for profit.

mills
Buildings where raw materials are turned into products.

padrone
An employer who takes advantage of immigrant workers, particularly Italian immigrants.

petition
A formal request to a higher authority signed by many people.

reforms
Changes put in place to improve or fix problems.

respiratory
Relating to the act of breathing.

steerage
The lower deck of a ship, assigned to passengers with the cheapest tickets.

strike
When people stop working as a way to demand better working conditions or better pay.

textile
Relating to fabric or weaving.

ventilated
Allowing fresh air to enter and move through a room or building.

TO LEARN MORE

BOOKS

Gray, Leon. *Horrible Jobs of the Industrial Revolution.* New York: Gareth Stevens Publishing, 2014.

Hubbard, Ben. *Stories of Women during the Industrial Revolution: Changing Roles, Changing Lives.* Chicago: Heinemann Raintree, 2015.

Mullenbach, Cheryl. *The Industrial Revolution for Kids.* Chicago: Chicago Review Press, 2014.

NOTE TO EDUCATORS

Visit **www.focusreaders.com** to find lesson plans, activities, links, and other resources related to this title.

INDEX

Answer Key: 1. Answers will vary; **2.** Answers will vary; **3.** C; **4.** A